**ROOTS AND RHYTHMS**

ROOTS AND RHYTHMS

# ROOTS and RHYTHMS

JAMAICA'S NATIONAL DANCE THEATRE

TEXT BY REX NETTLEFORD

PHOTOGRAPHS BY MARIA LaYACONA

ANDRE DEUTSCH

FOR THE DANCERS

FIRST PUBLISHED 1969 BY
ANDRE DEUTSCH LIMITED
105 GREAT RUSSELL STREET
LONDON WC1
COPYRIGHT © 1969 BY REX NETTLEFORD
AND MARIA LAYACONA
ALL RIGHTS RESERVED
PRINTED IN HONG KONG
BY TOPPAN PRINTING CO (HK) LTD
233 96126 9

Book and jacket designed by Maria LaYacona

This book was produced with the kind co-operation
of the artists and Managing Committee of the
National Dance Theatre Company of Jamaica Limited

# CONTENTS

| | |
|---|---|
| Foreword | 7 |
| **REPERTOIRE 1962—1964** | 8—27 |
| I  The NDTC — Its nature and image | 28 |
| II  Beginnings and objectives | 29 |
| III  Training and the trainers | 30 |
| IV  The dances and their relevance | 32 |
| **REPERTOIRE 1964—1967** | 36—93 |
| V  The music and musicians | 94 |
| VI  The dancers and their talents | 95 |
| **CHOREOGRAPHERS AND ARTISTS** | 97—108 |
| VII  Other major contributors | 110 |
| VIII  The audience and the critics | |
| Problems and the future | 112 |
| **REPERTOIRE 1968** | 114—125 |
| Repertoire — Listings  1962 — 1968 | 126 |
| About the authors | 128 |
| Acknowledgements | 128 |

## MESSAGE FROM THE HON EDWARD SEAGA

Minister of Finance and Planning, Jamaica

The National Dance Theatre Company has become such an integral part of the cultural scene in Jamaica that it is difficult to believe that it has been in existence for a mere seven years. In that time, the Company has established itself as a vital, young group of dancers whose enthusiasm, imaginative choreography, and standards of excellence have won them an enviable reputation whenever and wherever they have performed.

Perhaps the most commendable aspect of the National Dance Theatre Company's seven years of existence, however, is that, recognizing the limited resources of a developing country, they have succeeded in establishing and maintaining themselves without benefit of public funds. This has been achieved by the real sense of dedication which characterizes the entire group, all of whom are constantly making great sacrifices of time and effort to ensure that a high standard of performance is maintained. The results, as we who have seen them know, are exciting.

Government has, of course, on occasion financed overseas tours of the Company when they have been invited to represent Jamaica on a national level, such as the Stratford Festival in Ontario in 1963, the Commonwealth Arts Festival in 1965 and Expo '67 in 1967. Such support, however, might be regarded as Government's recognition of the level of excellence which the Company has achieved on its own efforts and in a remarkably short period of time.

By the very nature of their appreciation of the country's limited resources and the success which they have achieved on their own efforts, the National Dance Theatre Company can be regarded as a National Company in the very real sense of the word. I have great confidence in their future.

*Edward Seaga*

# FOREWORD BY PETER WILLIAMS

Editor of *Dance and Dancers*

Why do people dance? It's an atavistic impulse inherent in man — an expression of happiness, of sorrow, of aggression, of victory or just a natural reaction to a rhythm of life which takes on the character of its geographical climate. Anglo-Saxons, for instance, move in a more calculated manner and, because of their background, submit more readily to certain disciplines than do Africans. The nearer to the equator, the less inhibited and more impulsive movement becomes, with bodies reacting instinctively to rhythms and situations.

If dance was originally associated with some form of ritual, then it was only a natural step on from there for it to move into a theatre situation. Placed in this context it is necessary that those who form dance companies should use the whole ethnic back-cloth of their particular region as the basic foundation of their work. This is the first consideration; and then gradually, over a period of time, other forms, other disciplines, other schools can be imposed. What is vital is that those precious roots must never be destroyed, but must be nurtured and fed with whatever stimulant seems best suited for strengthening their natural growth.

This attitude, Rex Nettleford and Eddy Thomas brought to the Jamaican National Dance Theatre when they formed it in 1962. Both of them had a sound practical and intellectual knowledge of the various recognised schools of dance — of the classical academic technique, of the Martha Graham contemporary dance, of the Central European expressive dance — and what was important was to see how this could be applied to a West Indian movement pattern which up to then hardly existed in any particular disciplined form.

Not only was there this problem of developing a style, but also that of getting over to the Jamaican people the feeling that there was a need for such an artistic expression. Although there was probably the kind of resistance inherent in almost every country, this break-through was made easier owing to the fact that there was nothing to break down. In a developing country with no great dance traditions, the dancers and the public can all grow up together. Of course we all respect tradition, and dance tradition is particularly important because it has made the international language that has been built up through the centuries and which can speak to the entire world. In countries steeped in tradition it is sometimes very hard to move in fresh paths without breaking down those beliefs which people have been brought up to accept as the only way. It needs new eyes to see how the past can be used so as to move in the future.

These new eyes belonged to Nettleford and Thomas' who managed to use their experience in a form of dance theatre that reflected the climate of the Caribbean and was acceptable to the Jamaican people. It was also acceptable to Britain when the Jamaican National Dance Theatre appeared in the Commonwealth Festival of 1965. Then the company was only three years old and it seemed remarkable that in such a short time it could have achieved a cohesive mixture of folklore and more contemporary attitudes, especially when the artists were non-professional. But they were 'non-professional' in name only, because the whole company, who rehearse after doing their ordinary daily jobs, brought a finish to their work which might well put many a recognised professional company to shame.

It would seem that the Jamaican National Dance Theatre has found a way of moving that should provide the blueprint for the way in which all dance companies in developing areas might move if they believe that dance can speak in a language for all the peoples of this world. This is something vitally important, because already past experience has taught us that dance can break down barriers which keep nations from understanding each other, thereby helping to dissolve many of the troubles which beset this earth.

POCOMANIA

**POCOMANIA**

Barry Moncrieffe
Rex Nettleford
Audley Butler
and
Company

# LEGEND OF LOVERS' LEAP

Monica McGowan
Eddy Thomas

Bert Rose
Audley Butler

Eddy Thomas
Monica McGowan

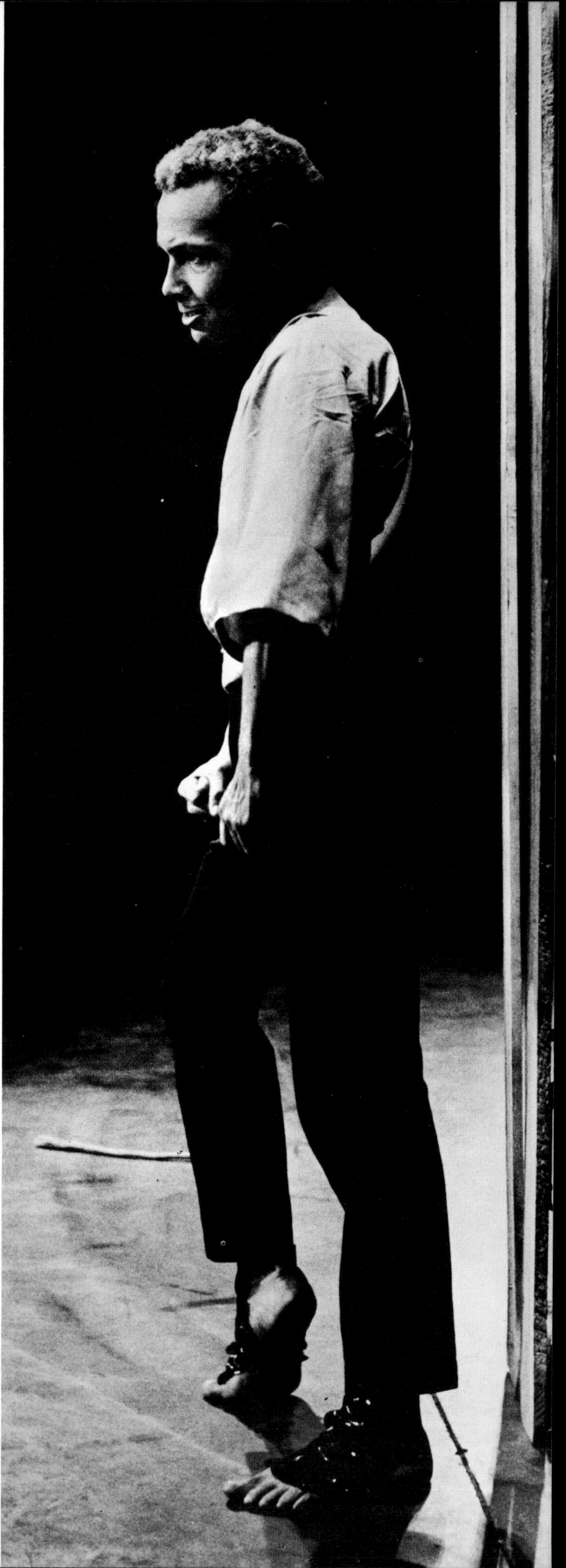

Audley Butler
Monica McGowan
Eddy Thomas                                    Bert Rose

Monica McGowan
Maureen Casserly
Bert Rose
Bridget Casserly

Eddy Thomas
Joyce Campbell
Barbara Requa
Rosalie Markes

# GAMES OF ARMS

Yvonne daCosta
Bridget Casserly
Audley Butler

Audley Butler
Rex Nettleford

Barry Moncrieffe
Patsy Ricketts
Barbara Requa
Carol Miller
Rex Nettleford

Bridget Casserly
Bert Rose
and
Company

## DIALOGUE FOR THREE

Eddy Thomas
Noelle Chutkan
Yvonne daCosta

Eddy Thomas
Sheila Barnett
Yvonne daCosta

27

Bert Rose
Bridget Casserly
Barbara Requa

Gertrude Sherwood

## I

*'Jamaica's National Dance Theatre last night offered a great deal of pleasure and one small problem. The problem is how to define them. Not really folk dancers, although they began their programme with traditional dances of exceptional subtlety and variety. Not strictly a ballet or modern dance company either, even though their dance dramas of a matrimonial triangle or a tragic plantation love affair are moving, direct and powerful. Perhaps best to just to stick to their own definition of "dance theatre" . . . .'*

It is natural for Jamaica's National Dance Theatre to present this kind of problem. This was not the only London critique which found the unsuccessful quest for a label disconcerting, though the Jamaica NDTC won critical praise for what was regarded at the 1965 Commonwealth Arts Festival as genuine achievement by a fledgling company. The Festival was indeed devised to display the common bonds as well as to share the wealth of diverse cultural strands. But it was quite understandable that metropolitan London, despite its sophistication, should betray uneasiness at the 'unusual' offerings from the outposts of an erstwhile empire.

In fairness, the *Times* of London had this to say: 'If the title of the National Dance Theatre Company of Jamaica sounds solemn or pretentious this is misleading, for the company is anything but solemn and not in the least pretentious. The key to all its work is an original and distinctive mixture of innocence and sophistication'.

Audiences in Cardiff, Coventry, Liverpool, Bournemouth and London itself also gave enthusiastic response from capacity-filled stalls, which delighted the Jamaican dancers. Morning newspapers generally gave high praise to the dancers' vitality, charm and gaiety, to their discipline and professionalism despite their amateur status and to the intelligence of the Company's choreographers and directors. In most cases initial response betrayed surprise at the range of the company. The 'variety of their dance styles,' the 'diversified dance programme' came in for comment everywhere. There was suggested disapproval, as in the case of the *Daily Worker's* critic who rued the European and American influence on the Company's approach to choreography, and the *Observer's* critic was consistent in his coolness to all the Commonwealth offerings. But others conceded the point, picked up no doubt from the Jamaican company's programme notes, that Jamaica is after all a diversified and complex little country. One critic empathised with the Jamaicans' effort to produce unity out of 'such disparate elements' and another surmised the possibility of a 'whole new school of dance' coming out of the mixture of Caribbean movement and modern dance technique. Still another admitted that the rare mixture of modern dance and traditional movement and music added up to a 'fully rounded theatrical occasion'. Some others had no reservations—to them the mixture proved 'irresistible'. But still to a great many there was cause for wonder at the 'sharply broken image of the Company'. For there were the expected traditional Jamaican dances and music, 'but surprisingly there were also two ballets, one by each of the Company's artistic directors, that gave the company a sudden unexpectedly ambitious face.'

I should here pause to repeat the Company's past warnings: to the exoticist who merely wants his appetite whetted with writhing primitive bodies, the Jamaican dance company may very well prove a disappointment. To those with a genuine interest in dance and the opportunities it gives that remarkable instrument, the human body, to explore the hidden range of its expression, the Jamaican company might well prove to be something more than merely interesting. Much of what the Company aims at achieving was summed up by a Canadian critic when the Company, after just one year of existence, appeared at the Stratford Shakespearean Festival in Ontario in 1963. It read: 'When the inclusion of the Jamaican Company in the Festival was first announced, there seemed to be a quite widespread tendency to dismiss it as just another group of ethnic dancers. In the first performance at Stratford, these young people have established themselves as something much more important — a company of wide background and multiple traditions, producing highly creative work, not only in the dance itself but also in the field of costume design.' In 1965 the Jamaican Company was reminded, along with all its Commonwealth cousins not based in London, that the basic problem facing all the dance groups from the Commonwealth was that of moulding their indigenous cultural material into a style that makes it theatrically acceptable outside their own territory. Let me add, but quickly, that the challenge is as much — and more — to make that style theatrically acceptable in our own territory. But so much for how others see the Jamaican Company. How have the Jamaicans seen themselves?

## II

Like all serious artists the Jamaican dancers have given priority to work of intrinsic artistic merit rather than indulged the folksy exoticism which they know wide-eyed foreigners and chauvinistic patriots all too frequently demand. The ethos of the Company flowed from the nature of its environment, the experience of its members and the leadership available. They knew from the beginning that the road to discovery in the dance had to be journeyed by them and by no one else. So although they learn established techniques born of creative work and experience of other peoples, other places and other times, work in the Jamaican National Dance Theatre Company was pledged to move to the pulse of Jamaica. It is one thing to be universal in art, it is quite another to find the specifics on which to base one's work so as to make it speak beyond one's own shores as well as to as wide a cross-section of humanity within them.

From the beginning, the objectives of the National Dance Theatre Company reflected an awareness of the tasks involved. The Company exists firstly to provide a vehicle for well trained and talented dancers who wish to perform and create works of excellence: in other words, works of standards comparable to those found in any other part of the world; secondly to help widen an informed and critical Jamaican audience which will be responsive to works of excellence in the theatre arts; thirdly, to experiment with dance-forms and techniques of all kinds with a view to helping to develop a style and form which faithfully reflect the movement patterns of Jamaica and the Caribbean area; and finally to encourage and, where possible, conduct serious research into indigenous dance-forms in Jamaica and the Caribbean area. The objectives, far from being unrealistic, have flowed out of the experience of the years before 1962 when after three hundred years as a colony Jamaica gained her Independence from Britain. It was in 1962, at the time of Independence, that the Jamaica National Dance Theatre Company was formed. The occasion of its formation was symbolic enough: questions of identity, of national self-respect, of new nationhood, of freedom even, can be of as much concern to artists as to politicians and technocrats. In developing countries they (the artists) are usually numbered among the nation-builders, though they need not be the poets of the status quo. The time of formation of the NDTC was also a most propitious and practical one for the dance theatre as an art form. For it gave the Government reason to commission works of merit in the arts and to make this possible all available talent had to combine efforts and resources. The result was 'Roots and Rhythms', a dance show generously financed from public funds and open for all the trained dancers then available to participate in. The theme for the production came naturally out of the diverse strands in the Jamaican cultural complex and in dance-theatre terms these were to be found in existing classical ballet, modern creative dance and primitive and West Indian dance forms. In all idioms there had been hardliners firm in their postures — depending on their artistic predilections, their genuine aesthetic preferences and in some cases even on their class and skin colour. The years preceding had witnessed in the dance movement in Jamaica attempts and failures at fusion, schisms, standstills and even boredom. Both the ballet schools and the major creative dance studios had readymade dancers of technical proficiency who were finding limitations to improvement arising from the circumstances of their own groups.

Two major factors had, however, brought these dancers together before 1962. The first was the opportunity given to dancers by three Little Theatre Movement (LTM) 'pantomimes', which are the highly popular Jamaican folk musicals staged annually in Kingston. *Jamaica Way* (1959) *Carib Gold* (1960) and *Banana Boy* (1961) were vehicles for more creative dancing than ever before. Ideas of integrating dance into the storyline were floating around at the time and as choreographer, stager of musical numbers and director, I managed to get more than one's fair share of dance and dancers into those productions. The musicals kept these dancers drawn from different studios working together for the greater part of six months each year, and exposed them to a semi-professional situation of a long run and the need for sustained rehearsals. They also added dimensions to the dancers' sense of theatre and expanded their performing range. The second factor which helped in getting able dancers to work together was my having to direct and keep alive both the pioneer Ivy Baxter group and the newly formed Eddy Thomas Dance Workshop during the two year period immediately preceding Independence when both dance teachers were away from Jamaica.

The advanced dancers from both studios came to be trained together, and following on this was a cultural exchange tour to Howard University, Washington, DC in 1961. The obvious team to go was the one built up through the pantomimes and the classes. The dancers were drawn from the creative Dance groups, and the classical ballet studios, but the repertoire that went was the repertoire that had been built up by Ivy Baxter, creative dance pioneer, teacher and choreographer who has played a pivotal role in the development of Jamaican dance-theatre. She was the first to give form and purpose to the creative dance movement, the vehicle for the new dance expression which finds its cumulative effects in the Jamaican National Dance Theatre Company today.

The link with Ivy Baxter was provided by NDTC co-founders, Eddy Thomas and myself, who jointly directed the dance company for the first five years of its life. We had both been members of the Ivy Baxter group. We had worked along with other NDTC dancers like Sheila Barnett, Joyce and Shirley Campbell, Barbara Requa, Monica McGowan, Ronan Critchlow, Rosalie Markes, Gertrude Sherwood and Audley Butler at different stages of the life of the Baxter group. But Jamaican dance-theatre had always drawn to some extent, and still does, on the classical ballet tradition. Ivy Baxter had herself studied with pioneer Hazel Johnson, a Jamaican woman of means who with her musician sister presented versions of the classics with taste and integrity. She was obviously a tremendous force since most of the major ballet studios today are run by persons who came under her influence. So the Faye Simpson School of Ballet was to provide for the young NDTC Yvonne daCosta (now ballet mistress and a highly talented dancer), Pansy Hassan and Noelle Chutkan. Courtesy tutors were to be drawn from other ex-pupils of Hazel Johnson. The Misses Betty and Punky Rowe offer classes to a number of company members and Barbara Fonseca continues to maintain a backdrop of disciplined training by spearheading the programme of RAD courses. The Soohih School of Dance, which was started independently in the late forties by Anatole Soohih, a Russian emigré, provided the Company with two gifted dancers in Maureen and Bridget Casserly. The school is now run by Madame May Soohih, his Jamaican widow. Then there was the Gordon-Rumsey School which produced Mavis Stoppi. To round off this early and important membership the Eddy Thomas Dance Workshop provided Bert Rose and Barry Moncrieffe. With Eddy Thomas and myself as principal teachers, assisted by senior dancers of the NDTC, the Dance Workshop was to be for five years the main vehicle of preparation of dancers for the NDTC. The majority of the teachers earlier mentioned willingly participated in the 'Roots and Rhythms' Independence Show which scored immediate success with Jamaican audiences. The nucleus of dancers who carried the load of the show was to form the National Dance Theatre Company which received immediate blessing from the Ministry of Development and Welfare (now the Ministry of Finance and Planning). The NDTC can, then, be said to be the positive expression of all the valuable work that had gone before — much of it maintained and since developed, little of it wasted.

Earlier in 1962 communication between Eddy Thomas and myself had resulted in his return to Jamaica. He had been in New York studying at the Martha Graham School of Contemporary Dance on a scholarship and on a Jamaica Government Arts Council Award. This award was the result of his achievements in the Jamaican dance-theatre as composer, costume designer and dancer. He had in fact teamed up with Ivy Baxter to produce such early significant works as *Rat Passage* (for which he was composer), and *Seven Stages* in which he danced a principal rôle. He had also been leading boy in two successful Jamaican pantomimes. He composed the music for the musical *Once Upon a Seaweed* which the Baxter group performed in 1960 and he formed the Dance Workshop in 1958. In America he studied with many of the leading modern dance exponents at a summer school at Connecticut College and danced for one season in the Graham Company, as well as on Broadway, in the short run of the musical *Kwamina*. His London appearance with the NDTC in 1965 earned him the appraisal of having a personal approach to modern dance forms, a strong dramatic sense and a personal utterance.

### III

This personal utterance was to serve well in choreography and teaching. Eddy Thomas brought with him the strength of the Graham dance technique as well as his own adaptations which fitted into the Company's policy of emphasis on *training* and *experimentation*.

Jamaican dance teachers have always felt that the proverbial calypso vitality of sunny Jamaica could only be enhanced by proper preparation of the body through a disciplined approach. The classical ballet antecedents have already been mentioned. But the University of the West Indies had been pressed into service through its Extra Mural Department which offered summer schools in which concentrated work in techniques and composition was done. All members of the NDTC have been beneficiaries of the exercise. Beryl McBurnie, the high priestess of Eastern Caribbean dance-theatre, enriched the Jamaicans' knowledge of the Caribbean dance heritage. Lavinia Williams-Yarborough of Haiti was to become a frequent visiting tutor, bringing with her the emotive drum language and luxuriant dance lore of Haiti and transmitting the magic of ritual with telling effect. Her contribution is particularly significant for a people concerned with definitions of their heritage. Miss Williams' work on Haitian dance has provided a body of teachable and valid technique which has provided Jamaican dance-theatre with relevance, vitality and a knowledge of a 'musical' use of the drum. (One year Jean-Léon Destine, the Haitian dancer, was guest teacher.) Eyrick Darby, a Jamaican, had earlier returned from his studies at Jacob's Pillow in the USA to work with Ivy Baxter and the Jamaican dancers in the summer schools. Through them Jamaican dance-theatre received injections of concentrated training and lasting exposure to established techniques as well as to creative work done in other West Indian territories. Another important contribution is the work of Neville Black, a Jamaican from Port Antonio, who came for many summers and once brought the American Maggie Kast with him. He had gone to the United States and had studied dancing with Sybil Shearer in Chicago, with Charles Weidman and Jose Limon in New York, as well as at the Martha Graham School. Although he has had a long performing experience leading his own company and working with the University and Court Theatres in Chicago, Neville Black prefers teaching to performing. This he approaches with fanatic dedication whether he is teaching for the University Extra Mural Department in islands of the Leewards and Windwards or whether he is 'strengthening the backs' of NDTC members at the barre or 'articulating the feet' of the new NDTC recruits in centrework. He teaches a jazz technique as well, and this is invaluable for developing sharpness of movement and speed.

As a teacher my own approach to training has been by way of discovering for oneself and bending some of the fundamentals of established techniques to the needs of the Jamaican dancers, never underestimating the necessity of a well-tuned instrument or of such technical proficiencies as strength, kinesthetic awareness, coordination and flexibility. But I am at the same time ever conscious of the stifling effect that exaggerated emphasis on technique can have for the work the NDTC sets itself. In a sense each dance does create its own technique, making the search endless and the creative spirit self-generating. My classes are therefore approached with this in mind, in a commitment to a judicious balance between maintaining natural vitality and imposing indispensable control. The breaking down of choreographic statements into their component parts is itself an important source of technique-building and this exercise I have regarded as essential for a company that seeks to find its own expression in its own terms. And although one does not disregard the discoveries by others, one cannot at the same time settle for slavishly copying a Graham, a Humphrey or a Cechetti. Indeed one cannot afford slavishly to copy anyone, not even oneself.

Some Jamaican observers question the priority of technique (especially when that technique is imported) over *content*, and rightly insist that our first responsibility is to ourselves in Jamaica rather than to audiences in London and Montreal where the NDTC has performed. It is true that replacing European classical ballet technique with North American modern dance does not solve the problem of developing what one observer called a 'truly national form and institution'. But classical ballet and modern dance techniques have fundamentals to offer, and these the NDTC has not been foolish enough to ignore. There are such fundamentals as the relaxation-tension factor in movement, of the contraction-release complex, of the use of breath and the alternate surrender to and defiance of gravity which are common to all dancing. The human body has a limited range of expression—whether it be Jamaican, American or Brazilian; whether it be black, mongoloid, or Caucasian. And in this we can afford transplants in vital areas. Everybody walks, runs, leaps, hops, jumps, glides, and skips. The field of sports (from athletics through football to cricket) shares much in common with the dance on this level. We can motivate these forms of locomotion, if we like, so that wherever one is in the world, somehow the 'body remembers how to crawl with fear, burn with anger, ache with fatigue, kindle with power and success'. This offers an underlying unity for the art of dance, stretching across the geographical boundaries and defying racial barriers. But I must quickly concede the point that the Jamaican will conceive, understand and appreciate his dance, drama, painting and music primarily through the structure and specificity of his own endeavours. The essence of dance in Jamaica must come out of a genuine desire and a developed capacity to give form to *our* experience. And I readily assert that the form (technique) given to our dance-works cannot be reasonably given any force which is not its own.

We know then that like physics, or carpentry, a craft underlies the great art of dance. We know that this has to be learnt and developed and we understand the two processes to be inextricably bound up together. In this respect the question of which is the chicken, which the egg, is a very real one even if sometimes begged; and we are aware that the solutions must come from us. This period of discovering, of shaping, the form out of the content is conscious transition. The ostensible flux will disturb and even discourage those who want to see definitions in specific (i.e. national) terms emerge quickly. But it must be seen as a necessary phase and one that can be overcome, given the willingness of the artists to struggle with creativity and to escape the temptations of blindly imitating what is current in London, Moscow or New York. NDTC cannot pretend to have found a technique that is 'Jamaican', but a vocabulary based on movement patterns peculiar to us is bound to acquire a logic, albeit an elusive one, of its own. Already questions of dynamics, of line, of our own mental outlook on dance and of movement-quality are playing positive rôles in shaping what may emerge as a 'style'. The final flowering in form and content will take time.

IV

What does the Jamaican dance company dance about? Jamaican audiences now take for granted the varied fare they receive each year in the Company's annual Seasons of Dance presented at the Little Theatre in uptown Kingston. Herb Whittaker of the *Toronto Globe and Mail* described the Company as follows: 'The visitors from Jamaica aid greatly in stretching Stratford's boundaries for in one programme they contribute as much as three companies might.' One could hardly expect less from a country whose apparent unity disguises a chequered past of discovery by the Spaniards and conquest by the English, who settled and governed it with the aid of British administrators and planters as well as African slaves. The latter are the two elements which are strongest and although Chinese, East Indians and Lebanese were to come in later and add further diversity and richness to the heritage, it is the melody of Europe playing upon the rhythm of Africa that predominates. Add to this the latter-day incursions from a cacophonous and dynamic North America which is a mere one and a half air-hours away, and one gets the cultural amalgam that determines much of what is called 'art' in Jamaica. Against this background, the company has faced critics who sometimes betray decided views on what elements should be selected from the heritage in order to produce a truly 'Jamaican' repertoire. This kind of difference in point of view is likely to turn on more fundamental problems of the nature and purpose of art and of dance in particular.

The folklore of Jamaica abounds not so much in movement as in songs and stories. Jamaican dance creators have therefore plunged adventurously into the creative and the abstract, making dances out of universal ideas and composing ballets out of the spirit rather than the letter of Jamaican folklore. This has led to exploration rather than to the boldly authentic commercialised transference from the field on to the stage. The exploration has produced a repertoire which is as varied as life in Jamaica itself. An editorial in the island's daily newspaper, the *Gleaner*, summed it up accordingly: 'The repertoire looks into the past at the plantation revelries without rancour, embraces pattern dances of the era; includes old legends represented in up-to-the-minute terms. It looks at the present in its amusing treatments of local life. It extends to what is termed pure dance in such items as its exploration of the eternal triangle or in lively interpretation of the musical scores chosen. It comments in a light-hearted way on such grave problems as the dangerous rivalry between powerful nations.' The above refers to such pieces as *Legend of Lovers' Leap* which deals with the master-slave relationship and is based on a legend popular in the parish of St Elizabeth and elsewhere. The slave period of Jamaica's history received lighter treatment in the 1963 production of *Plantation Revelry* with dances based on nineteenth century plantation rituals and customs. Here country dances, the traditional bucking fight, calembe, set girls (blues and reds) and John Canoe are placed in a setting of gaiety and abandon. Miss Amelia, a free-coloured scion of the plantocracy, returns from finishing school in England to joyous welcome. The literary and pictorial records in the Institute of Jamaica were invaluable for the creation of this work.

Jamaican folklife is depicted throughout the repertoire. There are *Country Wedding*, *Parade*

*Kingston 13, Pocomania* (a staged ritual), *Afro-West Indian Suite* and *Folkform* depicting the sheer joy of movement in the folk tradition; there are *Jamaican Promenade, Night Shelter* and *Kas Kas* which depicts the humour that is to be found always in a Jamaican urban backyard. It is one of those backyards which have reason to keep the police at arms' length or to get them to yield to the temptation of drink and feminine flirtation. *Night Shelter* provided straight entertainment by breaking the no-males-allowed rule which obtained in the old Friday night penny-shelters in Kingston of yesteryear. *Parade Kingston 13* commented on typical situations of the less privileged in a vital zone of the nation's capital. Even when dances make their so-called 'social comments' the emphasis on the folk contribution has produced fun, entertainment, uninhibited humour. This has pleased most people, but some 'serious' Jamaicans have taken umbrage at the way 'our' material has been lightly treated.

In 1964 the Company essayed a serious treatment of Jamaican life in *Two Drums for Babylon*. Its point of take-off was the Jamaican cargo cult of Ras Tafari and the work made its point in respect of the class conflict and value contradictions which abound in the island today. It is a young middle-class boy who is attracted by the 'phantom forces' of the Rastafarian cult. His betrothed pursues him into the camp, followed by her three attendants — middle-class ladies of quality, all. The Rasta Chief is a kind of father figure to the boy, who has second thoughts when the girl enters the camp and becomes involved with the Cult leader. Jamaican critics voted it the 'most genuinely interesting ballet' of the season and one gave it 'two cheers' after a second viewing, but only after a second viewing. Maturity of thought and execution was praised and the work did indeed break new ground in movement patterns and invention for the dancers and for at least one choreographer.

Jamaican content in the NDTC repertoire is not always as obvious as is suggested in the works above. *Games of Arms* takes its theme from the global arena of power politics but the mixture of sophistication and innocence in its conception and portrayal gives it a special Jamaican feeling. It is the Jamaican schoolyard experience with its gauche and childlike jumps and leaps and skips which gave the choreographer his point of departure. The futility of the global arms race and journey towards annihilation could well be Jamaica's point of view among the coterie of small nations whose commitment to survival is a real thing. *Dialogue for Three* like *Game of Arms* transcends territorial borders but it is a distillation of experience relevant to us. Though it is usually lauded on the superficial level of a simple intriguing affair between a man, his mistress and his wife (and this is everywhere) the ballet seeks to underscore the dominance of the woman in Jamaican society. The dominance is rooted both in matriarchal power over husbands and sons and in the compassionate understanding that women seem to have between each other in the matter of loving the same man. The need for a child — a cultural necessity in a country where to be barren is to be cursed — is also important to the unfolding of the dance-drama in *Dialogue*. *Masques of God* develops much of the theme introduced in *Dialogue*. Here it is not only matriarchy but the feminine nature of Jamaican society which is dealt with. The flight from responsibility (in this case, from family responsibility) by the young man in *Masques* is something which, if not peculiar to Jamaica, is too well-known for further comment; so are the Anancy figure (Clown) and the frustrated spinster. No less contemporary is the treatment of the population explosion problem in *Omegan Procession*. The opening passage has its inherent plastic virtues in pure dance terms but it is the Garden of Eden — the myth of Creation which Christian Jamaica knows and believes in. The final curtain catches the process of procreation starting all over again; and above the goings-on, unborn foetuses struggle for survival through an ornamental coil. The 1968 Season saw the creation of *The 'King' Must Die*, a ballet about the penalty of power — the logic of people needing 'Messiahs', enthroning them, then killing them in one form or another. It comes directly out of the Jamaican experience but has its universal application particularly in respect of the quality of political violence in the contemporary world.

Both *Games of Arms* and *Dialogue for Three* could be said to have established the Company as a serious artistic endeavour in international terms. The *Times* of London said *Games* was 'as effective and original in execution as in conception'. The simple expressiveness of Eddy Thomas's choreography had connected, as it were. *Dialogue for Three* was praised for its 'unique dignity and sensuousness'. Initial response to this work in Jamaica back in 1963 betrayed doubts on the part of at least one major critic, but this was soon to transform itself into high critical approval for choreographic conception and execution by various casts. Today the work has become a kind of perennial in the repertoire with frequent changes of cast, and something of a challenge to all principal dancers who aspire to integrate dramatic interpretation with technical proficiency. *Masques of God*, choreographed in 1966 and which has never been shown outside Jamaica, also presents serious challenges for principal dancers in the Company. Though not intended as psycho-drama, it presented challenges to critics who seemed disturbed by the 'symbolic and allegorical subtleties' and by its 'intellectualism'. The dancing by the Company was, however, praised for its tautness and cleanness of line and 'moments of beauty' were conceded, as indeed they also were in *Omegan Procession* which was mounted the same season. *The 'King' Must Die* (1968) was said to be a major work of importance and one critic thanked Providence that the choreographer had broken away from what she termed the 'Nettleford choreography'. The occasional elements of 'daring and surprise' mentioned was probably the cause for the hesitancy displayed by two other critics who plainly said that they would have to view the work a second time in order to make up their minds. As one put it: 'I am not going to attempt fully to review *The 'King' Must Die* from a single viewing. I have been too wrong on similar occasions with regard to his (the choreographer's) more ambitious ballets'; though he said he found the 'theory' behind the scenario 'interesting'.

Religion is something central to Jamaican existence. The NDTC repertoire responds naturally. *Pocomania*, a Jamaican folk worship, is danced not as a send-up of subculture cultism but as a serious experience. *And It Came to Pass* is said to match the beauty and simplicity of the story of the Nativity. *Misa Criolla* is a choreographed ritual of the religious experience (this time the Passion). Some critics felt it was not reverent enough. The conventional European symbols were probably given too much vigour and brought too close to earth. But its creation was prompted as much by a desire to give form to the experience of rejecting conventional modes of worship as by the wish to highlight the basic similarities in all worship. It had the honour of being performed along with the *Bach Chorale* and *Ave Verum* in the history-making church service in the Scots Kirk, Kingston, at Easter of 1968. And it was a revelation to see how these works assumed proportions of aesthetic propriety and even suggestions of grandeur in their 'natural setting'. On December 10, 1968, a re-worked version by Neville Black of the *Bach Chorale* was presented as part of the national ceremony when Jamaica made a posthumous award of the Marcus Garvey Prize for Human Rights to the late Martin Luther King, Jr. Also on the programme was a dedicatory sequence danced to the Negro spiritual *Every Time I Feel The Spirit*.

The Afro-content of works in the NDTC repertoire is something of obvious sociological and psychological import. Ninety per cent of the Jamaican population are of African descent. Happily it also offers the kind of interest and quality that makes dance-theatre vital and stimulating on its own terms. *African Scenario* seeks to dig up much of our roots and to celebrate many rhythms which are extant in Jamaican dance lore — for example Kumina, Pocomania, John Canoe, Etu and Burroo. When the work was first performed it evoked favourable responses from many Jamaicans, though some people felt that middle-class restraint had imposed itself on the bodies of the dancers, male and female alike. At least one viewer walked out of the Little Theatre in disgust — all that 'belly-rolling and back-to-Africa nonsense'. A few complained that the drumming was too much for them. The work was the result of a visit by me in 1962 to West Africa where I had renewed acquaintances in classes and repertoire sessions with Beryl Kari-Kari and the Obadjeng Dance Group in Accra, Ghana, and with Opoku in Kumasi, as well as with dancing 'societies' in Nigeria. Parallels with movement patterns in Jamaica and Haiti were self-evident: admittedly one was inspired. The approach to *African Scenario* was ritualistic and frankly theatrical — thanks to the usual collaboration of Eddy Thomas on costumes. But the work carried undercurrents of identity with Africa and this disturbed some people among the Jamaican audiences.

As a dance company the NDTC concerns itself with developing its vocabulary in terms of such dance concepts as space, time, rhythm, dynamics and form. *Footnotes in Jazz, Concert Suite, Dance Andante, Rites, Waltz Suite, Sonata, Foiled Encounter, Homecoming* all explore in some way movement for its own sake. This is a valid and necessary exercise for any serious dance company. Works like *Rites* and *Homecoming* go beyond this in their own theatrical eloquence but they, along with others, present the dance artist (performer and creator) with challenges of technical expression and range which can indeed be pressed into the service of the so-called 'relevant' works. The 1968 season added richly to the repertoire Neville Black's *Legendary Landscape* and *Bach, Brubeck and Company*, as well as Sheila Barnett's *Ring Hunt*. They tell their own stories in terms of dance dealing with themes of life and death, the jazz form itself, and the inescapable commitments of the male-female relationship. They add to or deepen the company's vocabulary in pure dance terms. In this sense, *Legendary Landscape*, danced to an electronic score, is a truly significant contribution to NDTC's life. The Jamaican critics warmed to it and one voted it the 'hit of the season'. But it was the pure movement quality and choreographic skill of the *Bach, Brubeck* piece that won widespread audience appeal. *Fables,* based on the James Thurber stories, adds a dimension of acting which is essential to the dance-theatre artist and though some critics insist that Anancy stories, which are Jamaica's folktales, should take precedence over Thurber's tales, which are American, the exercise presents challenges to the dancers as artists, and they give enjoyment.

The choreographers responsible for most of these works have been Eddy Thomas, Sheila Barnett, Neville Black and myself. Eddy Thomas's lyricism and personal approach to modern dance forms won acclaim from *Dance and Dancers* which described him as a 'notable choreographer of modern dramatic works'. He is strongly influenced by music, always seeking to reconcile movement pattern with musical phrase without enslaving his dancers in the body of the measures. His concern with line, lyric quality and his sense of detail in shaping a movement pattern are all evident in such works as *And It Came to Pass* and *Omegan Procession* of 1966 — his most recent work for the company.

His genuine theatrical flair is always evident and his skill at costume designing helps not a little in heightening this. *Games of Arms* demonstrated his sense of comedy and capacity to explore humour in choreographic terms.

It is to Neville Black that one looks for dance humour, however. His use of isolations and distortions of movement patterns never fails to surprise, and his natural sense of comedy comes out even in his 'serious' jazz works. He sees jazz as an ideal dance form to express humour. He is noted for his skilful use of modern dance forms in their economy, neatness of construction and effective sense of design and this evoked praise from *Dance and Dancers* referring to his work *Rites*. Although he seemingly depends on music for his inspiration, he is known to begin works long before he has 'found his music' and one of his latest works, to an electronic score, was something of a celebration of movement on its own terms. His spatial designs are peculiar to him, and although he sometimes betrays commitment to certain academic ideals in shaping a movement he never stops experimenting, whether he is spiralling a dancer into a spectacular fall or counterpointing arms against feet against pelvic region.

Sheila Barnett is sometimes said to be cerebral. Ever since she did *Jazz Fantasia* she has exhibited the care and attention to details and nuances that come from her occupation as a teacher who trains on the basis of fundamental movement principles. But she never sacrifices quality of movement to achieve what she wants. She uses space with assurance and designs shapes with a plastic awareness that has won her critical acclaim for her work with *Ring Hunt*. Jamaican critics are all unanimous in their praise of her musical sense and her singular preference for using music as an extra dimension to the dance rather than relating dance to music in 'overt interpretative patterns'.

As for myself, it is naturally difficult to talk about my own work in this way. But I can safely report that my choreographic approach is determined largely by my concern with rooting my work in the collective experience of the people I think I know — that is by distilling the essences and attempting to arrive at the universality in a particular experience. The process often results in concealing the connexion between a movement design born out of Jamaican folk forms and its distilled representation in my so-called 'serious' works. I have been described as 'intellectual in approach' — and there is no doubt about the importance of 'the idea' at the centre of such works as *Dialogue for Three, Two Drums for Babylon, Masques of God* or *The 'King' Must Die*. But the richness of ritual, the sheer joy of moving and the natural feel for theatre are constant elements in the quality of these very works as in the many Jamaican folk works which I have choreographed. It has been suggested that the shaping of movement patterns and the building up of a vocabulary in terms of our own dance experience and movement patterns underlie the strong dramatic content of the so-called 'Nettleford choreography' whether light or serious. In answer to a question put by *Dance and Dancers* in 1965 I said:

> 'Both Eddy Thomas and myself work in what is perhaps a rather strange way because we tend to conceive our dances in purely abstract terms — in terms of developing a movement pattern, building on it in an architectural way. Once we find the basic vocabulary, we have to apply this in some sort of literal way, the marrying of the literal and the abstract . . . .'

I have preferred to write scenarios from scratch rather than comment on someone else's story and I do struggle to make movement match theme in each separate endeavour. My work has been described variously as 'textured', 'imaginative', 'rhythmic'. It is this strong rhythmic sense that has sometimes been criticised as being the result of too much of a commitment to the use of the drum.

Beverly Kitson
Rex Nettleford
Patsy Ricketts

## PLANTATION REVELRY

Patsy Ricketts
Jackie Guy
Beverly Kitson

Bert Rose
Audley Butler
Rex Nettleford

Yvonne daCosta
Dennis Scott
Barbara Requa
Barry Moncrieffe

Dorothy Sanguinetti
Joyce Campbell
Bridget Casserly
Monica McGowan

PLANTATION REVELRY

# RITES

Audley Butler
Dennis Scott
Derek Williams

Mavis Stoppi

# DANSE JUBA

Barry Moncrieffe
Shirley Campbell

Monica McGowan
Rex Nettleford

# AND IT CAME TO PASS
Bert Rose
Sheila Barnett

Audley Butler
Ronan Critchlow
Dennis Scott

Derek Williams
Bert Rose
Barry Moncrieffe

Rex Nettleford
Audley Butler
Dennis Scott

Sheila Barnett
Bert Rose
Rex Nettleford
and
The Company

# FABLES

RED RIDING HOOD AND THE WOLF
THE UNICORN IN THE GARDEN
THE SEAL WHO BECAME FAMOUS

Carol Miller
Audley Butler

Neville Black

Pansy Hassan
Frank Ashley
Thomas Pinnock
Dennis Scott

**AVE VERUM**

Yvonne daCosta
Rex Nettleford

Recital in
Scots Kirk
Kingston
1968

# HOMECOMING

Sheila Barnett

**THE AWAKENING**

Noelle Chutkan
Eddy Thomas

## DANCE ANDANTE

Joyce Campbell
Barbara Requa
Sheila Barnett
Bridget Casserly
Yvonne daCosta
Monica McGowan

**PARADE, KINGSTON 13**

Audley Butler
Bert Rose
Rex Nettleford
Derek Williams
Thomas Pinnock
Rosalie Markes

Sheila Barnett
Joyce Campbell
Maureen Casserly
Monica McGowan

Derek Williams
Audley Butler
Bert Rose
Thomas Pinnock

# TWO DRUMS FOR BABYLON

Bert Rose
Bridget Casserly
Audley Butler

Milton Dawes
Thomas Pinnock
Derek Williams
Dennis Scott

Barry Moncrieffe
and
Company

Bridget Casserly
Noelle Chutkan
Yvonne daCosta
Mavis Stoppi

Audley Butler
Bridget Casserly
Bert Rose
Derek Williams
Dennis Scott
Thomas Pinnock

Audley Butler

# RECOLLECTION

Barbara Requa
Sheila Barnett
Yvonne daCosta

## DIARIST IN SAND

Eddy Thomas

# JAMAICAN PROMENADE

Bert Rose
Rex Nettleford
Audley Butler

Rex Nettleford

Gertrude Sherwood
Carol Miller
Pansy Hassan
Noelle Chutkan
Patsy Ricketts

Barbara Requa
Yvonne daCosta
Sheila Barnett

Joyce Campbell
Bert Rose
Rex Nettleford
Audley Butler
Thomas Pinnock

## KAS KAS

Rex Nettleford
Shirley Campbell
Sheila Barnett
Barbara Requa
Gertrude Sherwood
Yvonne daCosta
Patsy Ricketts

Joyce Campbell
Rex Nettleford

Thomas Pinnock and Company

**MISA CRIOLLA**

Bert Rose
Derek Williams
Barry Moncrieffe
in
KYRIE

Yvonne dCosta
Barbara Requa
Patsy Ricketts
Bridget Casserly
Monica McGowan
Gertrude Sherwood
in
GLORIA

Bridget Casserly
Yvonne daCosta
Patsy Ricketts
in
CREDO

Eddy Thomas and Company in SANCTUS

Eddy Thomas
Derek Williams
Audley Butler
Dennis Scott
in
AGNUS DEI

# COUNTRY WEDDING

Rex Nettleford
Barbara Requa
and
Company

## NIGHT SHELTER

Gertrude Sherwood
Carol Miller
Barbara Requa
Jean Binns
Pansy Hassan

# MASQUES OF GOD

Yvonne daCosta
Audley Butler

Audley Butler
Joyce Campbell
Thomas Pinnock
Bert Rose
Derek Williams
Barry Moncrieffe
Yvonne daCosta
Patsy Ricketts

Barry Moncrieffe
*as the Clown*

Gertrude Sherwood
Bert Rose

Sheila Barnett
and
Company

# OMEGAN PROCESSION

Sheila Barnett
Audley Butler

Yvonne daCosta
Audley Butler

Gertrude Sherwood

## WEST INDIAN SUITE

BANDANA DANCE
GEE BONGO LAY
SANTA FOULLE

Noelle Chutkan
Joyce Campbell
Sheila Barnett
Yvonne daCosta

Barry Moncrieffe
Audley Butler
Rex Nettleford
Derek Williams
Bert Rose

Shirley Campbell
Maureen Casserly
Monica McGowan

BANDANA DANCE

# AFRICAN SCENARIO
## INITIATION, BETROTHAL, WAR-FETISH, MASQUERADE

Gertrude Sherwood
Audley Butler

Barbara Requa
Joyce Campbell
Monica McGowan
Rosalie Markes
Sheila Barnett
Yvonne daCosta
Shirley Campbell

Dennis Scott
Thomas Pinnock
Audley Butler
Milton Dawes
Eddy Thomas
Bert Rose

Rosalie Markes

Rosalie Markes
Eddy Thomas

Audley Butler
Bert Rose
Thomas Pinnock
Barry Moncrieffe
Dennis Scott
Milton Dawes
Eddy Thomas

## V

The matter of the drum as a dominant musical accompaniment to the NDTC has been a matter of concern among some Jamaican members of our audiences. The NDTC has been fighting since 1962 the prejudices of some of our people against the 'unsubtle instrument' — the drum. Others, as if to ease the conscience, insist that the NDTC dancers dance best when they dance to drums. There is something in the proclamation! For NDTC dancers do dance well to drums, as they ought to. One should hope that they dance as well to all sounds which are relevant to the Jamaican experience. As a hybrid people we do have a capacity to respond to much that meets the ear. This probably explains the propriety and artistic success of Darius Milhaud's 'Suite Provencal' and Joaquin Rodrigo's 'Guitar Concerto' for *And It Came to Pass* and *Dialogue for Three* respectively. The musicians are French and Spanish in that order but the Jamaican choreographers found a community of spirit with them. This is the validity of art, or is it? The ideal is, of course, to have Jamaican composers creating to the pulse and tonal experience of Jamaica. We came somewhat near to this with the music for *Legend of Lovers' Leap* and *Games of Arms*, which was composed by Jamaican Oswald Russell. As it happens, Mr Russell has been brought up in a strong tradition of European music. But he found common cause with the NDTC because he, too, is dedicated to discovering relevant forms. His collaboration was an important beginning cut short too soon by his departure for Europe, where he now lives. Since Mr Russell's departure the hunt for music suitable for choreographing 'serious' themes on Jamaican life takes us more often than we care to admit outside the society. Experiments have indeed been made with local limited resources. The musical scores for *Two Drums for Babylon* and for *Liza* (variations on a Jamaican folk theme) have been worthy but not altogether satisfactory, for example. The Jamaica School of Music is probably too young to provide the stuff that is needed. Trained musicians are in relative abundance in the society but they seem to prefer to perform and teach rather than to plunge adventurously into the frightening unknown of creativity. The NDTC is very conscious of this major problem and must take steps to correct it within its own limited resources. But as Pamela O'Gorman, a local music critic, has said '... the crux of the matter lies in the mesmeric pull of European cultural influences which absorb most Jamaicans' energies, against their barely-existent interest in their own music or any of the other Jamaican art forms such as painting or dance, for instance. The NDTC must wait patiently (Lord, how long?) for the Outsider in our midst: the creative musician who can break away from the examination-passing, biscuit-crunching atmosphere of middle-class respectability that at present holds the local serious musician in thrall.'

The choreographer, if not held in thrall, is certainly forced outside for much of his music. Bach, Hindemith, Prokofiev, Milhaud, Bartok, Rodrigo are familiar names with us. And so are Gershwin, Blakey, Brubeck, Dello Joio, Benton, Charlie Mingus and Copeland — who may be said to be geographically nearer home. Ariel Ramirez and Revueltas round off the impressive list which has served us well and has strengthened our international language. But the cry for local composers developing with the dance is a very real and constant one.

We cannot claim, either, to be totally well served by our musical arrangements even for the traditional work the Company does. Mapletoft Poulle gave years of valuable service to the dance movement and for sheer vitality and authenticity of sound he gave the dancers memorable moments of joy which they in turn transmitted to thousands. But the absence of musicians willing to work on the same basis of philanthropic service as choreographers and dancers has remained a defeating factor. Today the Musical Director is Majorie Whylie, a young Jamaican with a natural feel for the dynamics of dance music and a dedication that fits into the life-style of the Company. She works constantly with instrumentalists who have to be hired from the Military Band or from commercial dance bands. She gets support from drummer Carl Messado and Ronan Critchlow, the master drummer who improved his drumming with the famous Tiroro of Haiti and helps to devise drumscores for the NDTC.

The Company has utilised groups of singers from time to time. First it was the short-lived Canboulay Singers. Then it was the Frats Quintet, an internationally acclaimed group of Jamaican folksingers who drew tremendous applause on all the NDTC tours abroad. Now it is the NDTC Singers led by Joyce Lalor who has been vocal soloist to the Company since its inception. A worker in educational television by day, she devotes her evenings to rehearsals and recitals on choirs, in musicals, television shows and the NDTC. Her repertoire is wide and as a graduate of the London College of Music she finds herself at ease both with folksongs and the classics.

Canned music has now become acceptable in the field of professional dance and the NDTC is no longer embarrassed by having to use tapes for its modern works as we were in 1963 on the tour to Stratford, Ontario. I recall *Legend of Lovers' Leap* being orchestrated on the flight between Kingston and Toronto and a mere few hours were spent in rehearsing it under the direction of composer Oswald Russell. With the use of tape no longer taboo, the role of Baldwin Lennon as Sound Director is a very important one to the Company. He has transformed his hobby into an expertise which is essential to the NDTC in its performances. Live music, however, remains an imperative for the traditional work and an evening's programme utilises both canned music and live orchestra. The latter employs much of the rhythm of the drum — one of our lasting links with Africa as with our Caribbean neighbours. In the Beginning the Creator must have made the Drummer, an African saying goes.

## VI

Who are the people who dance these works? *Dance and Dancers* once declared that 'the dancers are well trained: some could take their places in any of the world's important companies'. They have indeed demonstrated to their countrymen that the approach to excellence turns not only on talent but on hard work — sustained and systematic. They work with no expectation of remuneration and although many of them are motivated by a belief in their country's capacity to make a contribution to the world of dance, none of them are victims of a blind chauvinism. For they understand the need for intrinsic merit and they have learnt to take in their stride the question-begging as to whether the NDTC is 'national', 'Jamaican enough' or even 'relevant'. They have persisted in their work, making the Company into probably the most disciplined among major theatre groups in the country. They are said to be able to turn in performances of professional quality despite their amateur status, and they have earned for themselves and the Company an international reputation with appearances at the Stratford Shakespearean Festival (1963), the Commonwealth Arts Festival (1965) when they appeared in five cities giving twenty performances in twenty-eight days in addition to television appearances, and in Montreal, Canada on the occasion of Expo '67 in 1967. Smaller units of dancers have also toured West Germany and Nassau, Bahamas in 1965, 1967 and 1968. Their appearances at home in annual seasons and inter-seasonal performances, as well as their tours abroad have been labelled professional. But they are all amateurs in the sense that they earn their living doing something else.

The Jamaican dancers pursue differing careers, thus bringing to the theatre a variegated experience which can be shaped into something rich and dynamic. The dance corps abound with teachers (university, training college, secondary and primary school), fashion designer and graphic artist, civil servants (with varying skills), a solicitor, a chemist, laboratory technicians, telephonists, secretaries, executive assistants and physical educators. After a hard day's work, they don their tights and leotards and 'relax' in hours of taxing discipline of their bodies in technique and choreography. Many of them teach in their own studios and mount their own shows.

There is no star system by policy. Artistic director and choreographers have taken many lead roles in major dances but the special qualities of all the dancers in the Company have been the essential source of strength. Sheila Barnett is turning more and more to choreography but she has won unqualified praise for her maturity in interpreting rôles, her nobility and natural grace as well as her innate intelligence and musical sense. After studying educational dance in the United Kingdom she returned home to teach in schools and training colleges and has made a contribution to dance-education in the island as a whole. She has created such memorable rôles as the Wife in *Dialogue for Three* and the Maiden in *And It Came to Pass*.

Yvonne daCosta, who is also ballet mistress, has many sound gifts that have rightly earned her a special place in the gallery of dance-theatre artists in the country. She has a wide technical range, being at home in primitive, folk and modern interpretative work. Her plasticity of form has made her the 'dancer's dancer' and she has danced in more dances than anyone else in the Company. Her musicality, sense of movement phasing and powers of concentration are assets for her performance of the difficult rôles she has created such as the calculating Other Woman in *Dialogue for Three*, the unfulfilled Spinster in *Masques of God*, and the dramatically dominant Queen Mother in *The 'King' Must Die*. In all three she has won high critical acclaim and she now tackles her rôles with that unparalleled depth and understanding which has increased her stature as a dancer, giving her a place of decided and well-earned eminence.

Audley Butler, the ballet master, is also a gifted dancer. He shares with Yvonne daCosta an almost impeccable ear for music skillfully used to memorise phrasing and time-space value of individual movements served up in the varied choreography. He possesses a magnificent presence and a special quality rooted in physical strength and a defined muscularity. He has created many major rôles in the Company's repertoire such as the Warrior in *African Scenario*, the Cult Leader in *Two Drums for Babylon*, Adam in *Omegan Procession*, the Brute Bachelor in *Masques of God* and the Usurper in *The 'King' Must Die*. His comic and acting talents are given full rein in *Games of Arms* and in *Fables*.

Bert Rose is technically strong and possesses outstanding dramatic ability and versatility. Described at home as a 'clean and lyrical dancer of very definite value', he was to earn praise from *Dance and Dancers* for his 'convincing projection of the dominant and decadent Plantation Owner' in *Legend of Lovers' Leap* and his 'striking performance' of the Boy in *Two Drums For Babylon*. *Ballet Today* praised his sensitivity. He was later to take over the rôle of the Man in *Dialogue for Three* at short notice in Nassau, later dancing it in the 1968 season to critical acclaim. He has studied on scholarship at the Graham School of Contemporary Dance in New York and has had performing experience on off Broadway. He made all the major tours with the NDTC and between 1959 and 1965 danced in all the dance shows and big musicals staged in Jamaica. His ambition is to teach, choreograph and design, as well as to continue performing.

Yet another remarkable dancer is Barry Moncrieffe, who has also studied in New York on scholarship at the Graham School and has lately won for himself much acclaim for his improved technical strength and the wonderful things he does with his naturally graceful and expressive limbs. His dedication, seriousness of approach and natural enjoyment of movement comes out in all his work and his performances as the Young Man in *Two Drums for Babylon* as lead dancer in *Bach, Brubeck and Company* as well as the masked Clown in *Masques of God* and a Revolutionary in *The 'King' Must Die* are all memorable ones among Jamaican audiences.

Barbara Requa did most of her dance training in Jamaica but she also studied educational dance in England. She has a natural elegance both on and off-stage which makes her a favourite with audiences in her native Jamaica. She received good notices for her portrayal ('like a flaunting Queen') of the Other Woman in *Dialogue for Three* and her charm and innate wit makes her a delightful exponent of Jamaican and Caribbean folk sequences (Bride in *Country Wedding*). She demonstrated talents as a commedienne in Jamaican musicals and in a local production of *The Boy Friend* in which she played Maisie with aplomb. She is a teacher by profession at one of Jamaica's leading Teacher Training Colleges and his incorporated dance into her physical education curriculum to advantage.

Gertrude Sherwood is a lab technician by profession but a dedicated and talented performer, being at home in a wide range of dance styles as demanded by the repertoire. While pursuing academic studies in London she worked with the famous ballet teacher Kathleen Crofton, rejoined the Company for the Commonwealth Arts Festival, then returned home to take a job, to dance, and to teach dance to her studio of toddlers. She won much praise for her work as the Initiate in *African Scenario* and has since created the rôle of Woman in *Omegan Procession* as well as resumed the rôle of the Wife in *Dialogue for Three*.

Derek Williams emerged as a dancer of promise when he took a featured part in *Rites*. His good lines, excellent physical proportions and other natural gifts were a good background for his journey to New York to study at the Martha Graham School on scholarship. He later became a trainee with the Harkness Ballet, gaining a place in the Youth Company, and went on to work with the incipient company based on the Harlem Arts Centre run by Arthur Mitchell of New York City Ballet. After a season's absence he returned for the interim show at the University of the West Indies Creative Arts Theatre featuring in *Bach, Brubeck and Company*.

Dennis Scott is a poet and a playwright besides being a dancer. After three years of concentrated and outstanding work of training with NDTC artistic co-Directors he became a full performing member of the Company, featuring in such works as *And It Came to Pass* (as the Carpenter) and *Rites*. He toured the UK with the Company where he danced the Plantation Owner in *Legend of Lovers' Leap* at short notice, and has since built up important rôles in some of the Company's major works. He alternates Adam in *Omegan Procession* as well as the Brute Bachelor in *Masques of God*. In 1968 he excelled as the lead dancer in *Legendary Landscape* and created for the season's programme a vignette called *Bread*. His technical strength and dance intelligence are his best assets.

Bridget Casserly sometimes brings to the dance that spirit of enquiry and alertness of mind which had made her a personality on the West Indian University Jamaica campus when she pursued a course in Economics (Honours).

*Continued on page 109*

**REX NETTLEFORD**
Artistic Director & Choreographer

**EDDY THOMAS**

Choreographer

**NEVILLE BLACK**

Choreographer

**YVONNE daCOSTA**

Balletmistress

**AUDLEY BUTLER**

Balletmaster

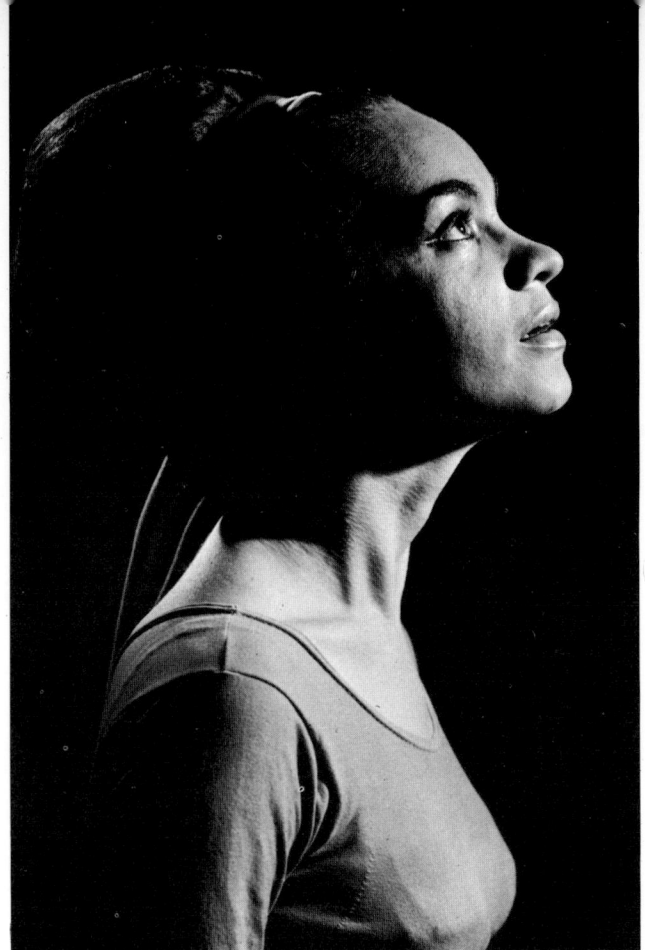

**BRIDGET CASSERLY**

**DEREK WILLIAMS**  **GERTRUDE SHERWOOD**

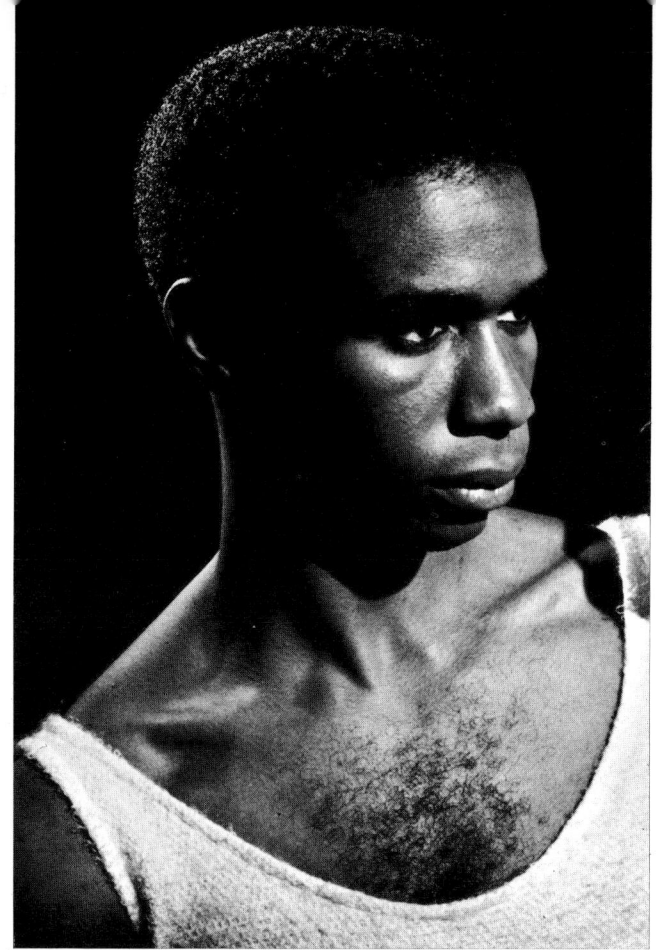

**BARRY MONCRIEFFE**

**BARBARA REQUA**

**BERT ROSE**

**NOELLE CHUTKAN**

**SHIRLEY CAMPBELL**

**MONICA McGOWAN**

PANSY HASSAN

JOYCE CAMPBELL

DENNIS SCOTT

THOMAS PINNOCK

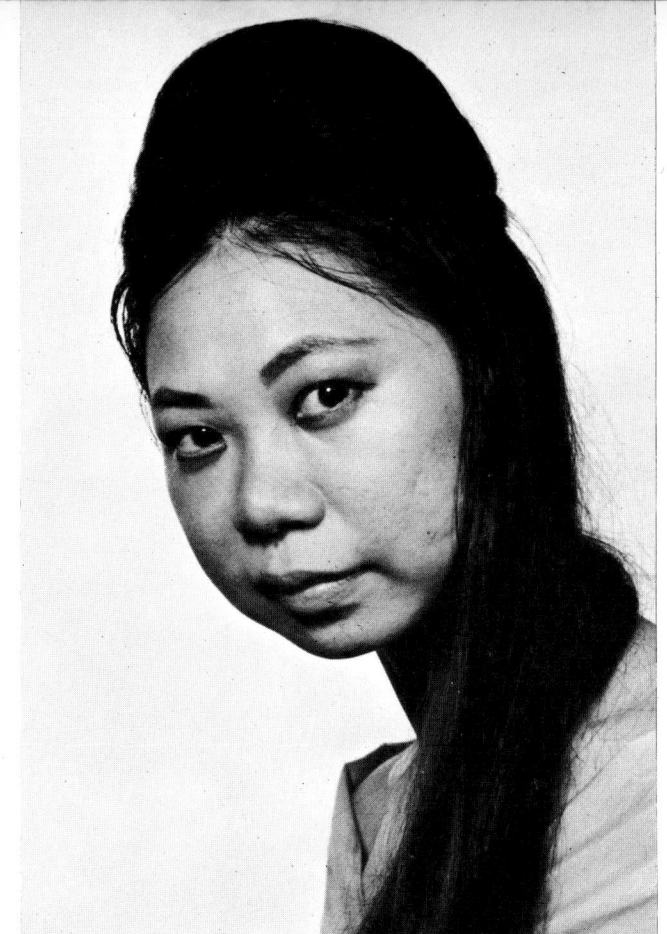

MAVIS STOPPI

PATSY RICKETTS

CAROL MILLER

DOROTHY SANGUINETTI
CHERYL RYMAN
JACKIE GUY
MADGE BRODERICK
JEAN BINNS
BEVERLY KITSON

**JOYCE LALOR**
Vocal Soloist

Vin James
Stan Irons
Paula Johnson
Carmen Gordon
Hazel Sinclair
Noel Heron

**RONAN CRITCHLOW**
Master Drummer

**MARJORIE WHYLIE**
Musical Director
and
Drummers

*Continued from page 96*

She has a good sense of interpretation and a lyrical quality that betrays her years of classical ballet training under Madame May Soohih. She dances the Young Woman in *Two Drums for Babylon* and is a featured dancer in the love-duet from *Games of Arms*, in 1968. When she is not dancing or studying she is said to be engaged in some political debate about the future of developing countries. She took over the rôle of the Wife in *Dialogue for Three* with success.

Joyce Campbell is known throughout the rural parts of Jamaica for her work in dance-education. As a Festival Officer (Dance) she helps to plan the dance offerings which increase yearly in the annual Jamaica Festival held at Independence anniversary time. She has had long experience in the Jamaican dance movement and has toured Trinidad, Cuba, Washington and Baltimore and Stratford, Canada. An expressive dancer with a good sense of mine and much acting ability, she got rave notices for her portrayal of the 'teggereg' in *Kas Kas* (1965) and won praise for her dancing in *Bach Brubeck and Company* (1968). A hard and dedicated worker, she leaves nothing to chance in anything she does. She dances in most of the Company's major works and recreated a Jamaican *quadrille* (traditional dance) for the Company in its 1964 Season. She also directs the Jayteens Dance Workshop, which has made several appearances on local television.

Noelle Chutkan is a quickwitted and theatrical dancer who has been on the Jamaican stage since she was a child. She brings to the dance an analytical approach and an enthusiasm which characterises her personality. She has good presence on stage and has won credits for her dramatic renditions of the Wife in *Dialogue for Three*. She is in fact a fine actress, having had experience in local drama groups. She has also participated in many Jamaican musical shows which gives her the self-confidence and assurance for which her dancing is noted.

Monica McGowan is a kindergarten teacher by profession and extends her love for working with children to a thriving dance school run at the Junior Centre, Kingston. She is, however, a very good performer with a strong technique, sense of style, dramatic ability and a feel for all aspects of the Company's repertoire. She is particularly gift at interpretation (as in the role of Liza in *Legend of Lovers' Leap*) and is capable of coquettish wit and charm as in *Juba*.

Thomas Pinnock is the 'funny boy' of the Company, excelling in rôles that call for humour (as the Thief in *Kas Kas*). But behind this is a strong technique further strengthened by his studies in New York. He has a natural feel for jazz and for the folk forms of his native Jamaica. He has real talent for mime and his sense of comedy is infectious, earning him a strong following among the Jamaican audiences.

Shirley Campbell has a winning stage personality and is a delightful exponent of dances which evoke gaiety and wit. She also danced the sensitive role of the Maiden in the 1964 Season in *And It Came to Pass*. She comes from the earlier days of the Jamaican creative dance movement and brings to her dancing self-confidence and dependability. She has toured Trinidad, Cuba, Washington/Baltimore and Stratford, Canada where she won critical praise for her portrayal of the Hen in *Gallandar la Pava* (Spanish West Indian Suite). In the 1968 Season she shone in the jazz work *Bach Brubeck and Company*.

Patsy Ricketts is a dancer with a striking personality on stage — an asset which has won her the attention of both Jamaican critics and audiences. She is developing a strong technique, a lyrical quality, sharpness of execution, clean lines and inborn stagecraft. She comes from a musical family, and her phrasing and musical sense are among her best assets. She served as a supporting dancer for one season, then joined the Company after the Commonwealth Arts Festival tour. She has since toured with the Company to Expo and dances parts in major ballets in the repertoire, excelling in *Ringhunt* and in the duet from *Bach, Brubeck and Company*.

Carol Miller loves to dance — that is one of the best things about her. But her developing technique has and made her one of NDTC's most reliable performers. She has great strength and speed and excelled in *The 'King' Must Die* as the female revolutionary, as well as in *Legendary Landscape*. She is also adept at jazz and folk-work and has an innate sense of humour which the NDTC has yet to explore to its fullest.

Pansy Hassan appeared with the Company at the outset in the 'Roots and Rhythms' Independence show in 1962, when she danced the rôle of Liza in *Legend of Lovers' Leap*, winning credits for her sensitive portrayal. Marriage took her away to the United States, where she continued studies. She returned in 1966 to appear in *Concert Suite* and *Masques of God* as the Wife.

Mavis Stoppi has a natural grace in her dancing and has used it to good advantage in a number of major works of the Company. She performs to greatest advantage in Neville Black's *Rites*. Her acting talents reveal a refreshing sense of comedy and she created the rôle of the dumb ballerina in a vignette for the 'Roots and Rhythms' season.

In 1968 many recruits were taken into the dancing corps of the Company. They had all studied with the company's artistic director and choreographers before attaining to full membership. Jean Binns whose dance-theatre experience dated back to an LTM pantomime of the late fifties was supporting dancer from 1965 to 1967, when she was promoted to Provisional Dancer status. She then toured Expo '67 with the Company, dancing in *Games of Arms* at short notice when ballet mistress Yvonne daCosta sustained a wrist injury. She sometimes works as a model and beauty consultant. Madge Broderick has been a supporting dancer with the NDTC since 1964, becoming a Provisional Dancer in 1967. Her theatre experience extends to LTM pantomimes and studio dance concerts and she is known for attack in performance. Fredericka Byfield owes her early training to Monica McGowan, a foundation member of the NDTC. She appeared with the company in the Scots Kirk Easter recital as a Provisional Dancer. Cheryl Ryman has many gifts: she has real talent for dance and drama. In 1967 she appeared with the NDTC as a supporting dancer and later worked with Neville Black for several television appearances. By Easter 1968 she was ready to appear with the company in the Scots Kirk recital.

Beverly Kitson, an American, is the second non-Jamaican to be admitted into the NDTC; the other was Nancy Epinat of Paris who worked with the Company in 1964. She comes from a strong background of training and performing in modern and classical ballet in the USA and the Philippines. She has successfully mastered the company's style, earning praise for her technical strength and assuredness.

Other dancers of real promise are Dorothy Sanguinetti and Andrea Anderson. Miss Sanguinetti has a natural sense of style and excels in dances calling for Jamaica folkmime and movement pattern. A hard worker, she has good co-ordination and is a reliable performer. She has previously appeared in LTM pantomimes and studio concerts. Miss Anderson's petite lyricism belies the fact that she is a hard-headed solicitor in normal life. Trained in the Soohih school in Jamaica, she is a good technician and possesses an innate sense and enjoyment of dance as well as natural beauty.

Male dancers are few and far between, as in most places. This puts heavy burdens on Jackie Guy, one of the Company's most enthusiastic apprentices. He studied with Alma Mock Yan and had performing experience with LTM pantomimes and in studio concerts. In 1968 he appeared with the company in the Scots Kirk recital and then toured Nassau, Bahamas. Frank Ashley has been on leave of absence from the company. He now studies in New York.

A few dancers have retired from dancing with the Company. They share the honours with those who remain for having helped to build dance-theatre to levels of excellence in the country. Maureen Casserly was a versatile dancer whose strong technical foundations and years of experience on the Jamaican stage turned her into a seasoned and polished performer with a great deal of musical sense and timing.

Ronan Critchlow, the master drummer, was the first male dancer of merit to emerge from the Jamaican creative dance movement some twelve years ago, creating the hero in *Rat Passage* (1954). He toured with Jamaican dance companies to Puerto Rico, Trinidad, Cuba, Washington/Baltimore and in 1963 to Stratford, Canada, with the NDTC and has taught dance in Jamaica, Antigua and Grenada.

Rosalie Markes, though married with a family of three children, found time to keep up her dancing which she began in her undergraduate days at the West Indian University. She betrayed in her dancing an 'inner sense of feeling' and projected serenity in her graceful carriage of the head.

Then there was Milton Dawes who created the rôle of the Carpenter in *And It Came to Pass* and toured with the Company to Expo', who left the Company when he migrated temporarily from Jamaica.

VII

There are blessings other than the dedicated service of the dancers. George Carter, the Lighting Director, is devoted to the work of the Company. A pioneer in lighting design since the early forties, George Carter has lit every major show presented in the island for wellnigh twenty years. He studied lighting in Britain on a Jamaica Government Arts Council Award, working with the Sadlers Wells Ballet, the Shakespeare Memorial Theatre at Stratford-upon-Avon, and the Welsh Opera Company. He also worked in the United States and manages an electroplating business in Kingston. The preparation of a season usually brings him together with Felix Barnett, a civil servant, and Freddie Hickling, a young doctor, who are the stage managers. Between them they have handled the Company's strenuous tours and have provided the settings in which the repertoire is annually mounted in Jamaica.

The free service by artists in related fields is yet another blessing. First it was Eugene Hyde and Milton Harley painting backdrops for *Dialogue for Three* and for *Games of Arms* respectively. Then one of Jamaica's folk-painters, Lloyd van Pitterson, did a backcloth for *Parade, Kingston 13*. But it was Howard Parchment, another Jamaican artist, who provided sculptured settings for *Masques of God*, the later mounting of *Dialogue for Three* and painted a backcloth for *Misa Criolla*. He was later to extend himself to costuming for *The 'King' Must Die*. The other contributing artist has been Moira Small who as an art teacher designed sets and backcloth for *Omegan Procession, West Indian Suite* and *Folkform*. She also designed the set for *Legendary Landscape* as well as costumes.

Costume designs have long been in the gifted hands of Eddy Thomas who has to his credit a long list of creations for most of the works in the repertoire. His sense of colour is considered among his greatest assets and his own knowledge of the dance has given him advantages over most other designers working in the theatre in Jamaica. Neville Black has also contributed designs with emphasis on line. So has Billy duMont whose *Rites* creations in 1968 replaced the ones which Neville Black had done for the original mounting.

The Wardrobe Mistress is Barbara Kaufman — reliable, even-tempered, dedicated and herself completely immersed in the art of dance, since she has studied dance in the Dance Workshop for many years and has performed in dance and musical shows for the past five years. She knows the importance of a costume to a dance and devotes herself tirelessly to the cause.

The work of photographer Maria LaYacona, a naturalised Jamaican of American stock, speaks for itself. But one must endorse what *Gleaner* columnist Barbara Gloudon once wrote: 'Credit for the Company's projection must also go to a particular person among the people backstage — a photographer, Maria LaYacona, whose sensitive studies of the dancers have appeared on posters, billboards, in other forms of advertising, on television, in the press and in dance publications of other countries. Today the LaYacona credit line and the NDTC have almost become synonymous.' Miss LaYacona humbly replied: 'Through the inspiration of the dance company I have benefited as a photographer.'

Art does beget art and NDTC's work has been a source of inspiration not only for photographers and dance-artists in the island but also for painters like Barry Watson, Alexander Cooper, Vernal Ruebens and Eugene Hyde, who once dedicated an entire exhibition to the subject of dance. The NDTC has been a source of inspiration not only to young aspirants in Jamaica but also to others in the English-speaking Caribbean. And Mervyn Morris, one of Jamaica's better-known poets, went home after a performance and wrote:

I
wounded
at home onstage
the wife betrayed lies
prone
arousing guilt

that other woman
regal in fading purple
wraps a sensuous leg

II
unmanned
in indecision he
berates the gods
that bid him choose

his clinging wife's fidelities
her tender reassuring flesh
domestic harmonies
the open breakfast face

or that sleek wanton queen
the red rose in her hair
who tightly as her loins clasp
asks nothing but
a fire to quench

III
balanced
in pain
his wanting body sweats

his manhood's hard

It is called 'Dialogue for Three' and is a consummate embrace of the spirit of the piece. The dancers he saw were Barbara Requa, Bridget Casserly and Bert Rose.

NDTC work has also produced at least two pieces of musical composition by Oswald Russell who includes a section of one of them, *Games of Arms*, in his own concert repertoire.

Behind all this is a conscientious Committee whose members also give of their time and service voluntarily. Headed by a young barrister, Joey Cools-Lartigue, assisted by Verona Ashman as Secretary, the Committee draws on a wide cross-section of interests. There are the practising artists in the Company on it but there is also a quantity surveyor (Maurice Stoppi), a businessman (Baldwin Lennon), a solicitor (Pat Rosseau), the founder of the Little Theatre Movement (Greta Fowler) and a producer and teacher of drama at the University (Noel Vaz). They work in between seasons to raise funds for mounting the Company's annual offerings.

Since 1962 three firms have 'sponsored' the season. In 1965 it was Rothmans of Pall Mall (Jamaica) Limited. In 1966 the Jamaican brewing firm of Desnoes and Geddes assisted, and in the year of Expo the Canadian-Jamaican alumina firm of Alcan Jamaica Limited gave an outright gift of money. The Company is plagued by lack of funds. Government support has up to now been restricted to grants for cultural tours abroad, though plans for a full-fledged training school could probably attract public funds. The device of 'Friends of the Company' has brought in some money but this, however helpful, is limited. Gate receipts from shows help substantially to cover costs of mounting. But the audience, though potentially large, is for the present mostly restricted to devotees who are regular theatre-goers.

## VIII

It is estimated that in Kingston the regular theatre audience numbers about six thousand out of a population of half a million. The NDTC has in fact had a wider audience, not only through television but also through its appearance on the Mona campus of the University, through its performances in town outside Kingston, as well as through its work for such special occasions as the recital in the Scots Kirk or participation in the Award ceremony on Human Rights Day when some four thousand persons in one sitting saw the Company perform. The choreographers and many of the dancers do have the added vehicle of the LTM pantomimes, Jamaica's most popular theatre-form playing to some sixty thousand people, annually. The core supporters of the NDTC are, however, the six thousand regulars already mentioned. Most of them will not have seen much dance-theatre, though over the years Jamaica has been exposed to those travelling pas-de-deux outfits backed up by a pianist accompanying and playing in the interludes. In more recent times full dance companies like Les Ballets Africains, Berioska, the Royal Winnipeg Ballet and the Australian Ballet and the Nederlands Dance Theatre have performed in Kingston to packed houses through the efforts of the Jamaican impresario Stephen Hill.

Many in a typical Jamaican dance-theatre audience will have travelled and will have seen or read something about the performing arts if not much of dance-theatre. This makes some of them fairly discriminating and sometimes very hard to please. The natural prejudices that seem to attend local offerings until they receive the seal of international approval have also plagued the Company, and NDTC's penchant for experimentation and breaking new ground has had its severe critics. I believe that this has come in part from many people's lack of security and confidence in themselves. This in turn breeds a suspicion for things local and a corresponding exaggerated respect for much that is foreign even when it is mediocre. Worse still, it breeds among many who regard themselves as educated a blasé philistinism that passes for sophistication and which is applied to discredit the work of the few who are really getting things done.

Yet the Jamaican audience have built up a discipline of appreciation of the NDTC's work. Some people insist on having all new works every season. While this wish is understandable, the danger in churning out a copious but frothy repertoire is very real. There is danger in a Company's repertoire growing too fast. Choreographers do not grow on trees in any cases, and the recently recommended short-term importation of American Negro choreographers is neither financially feasible nor necessarily a guarantee of any lasting or meaningful contribution to the artistic vision of the dance movement in this country. There is the added problem of familiarity breeding contempt in a society that is too small for escape. Dancers avoiding over-exposure by making themselves scarce before a season can help in preserving the illusion that is indispensable to the performing arts.

Yet on the whole the Jamaican audiences have been very sympathetic to the NDTC, though by no means over-indulgent. The refusal to take any and everything that is presented in the name of the dance is itself a welcome challenge to the NDTC, and on balance Jamaican audiences have been helpful. They have resisted new forms but they have also allowed themselves to be led and to accept some of the innovations — if only after three seasons. They can be readily sentimental about things which hit a responsive chord, as with *Dialogue for Three* and to a lesser extent *Legend of Lovers' Leap*. Anything for and with a laugh will have sustaining value and *Games of Arms*, *Kas Kas*, *Night Shelter* and the filler vignettes have had quick audience appeal.

The establishment of critics is very small in Jamaica. They are themselves amateurs, though they receive a token fee from the local newspapers which invite them to render their services. Heavy burdens are placed on them: they are required to write with authority about painting, ceramics, sculpture, drama, variety shows, soul music, films and of course dance.

Five newspapers employ the critics' services (including the *Sunday Gleaner*), and so do the two radio stations, which is to the lasting credit of the editors and programme directors of the news media. Like critics anywhere, those in Jamaica tear down, retract, encourage, ignore, needle and sometimes bend over backwards to please. As elsewhere, their criticisms too often reflect personal temperament rather than the art seen through such temperament. So it is quite natural for them to get into heated arguments — public and private but never violent — with some practising artists. The fraternal discord — for artists and critics are said to be brothers under the skin — is by no means unhealthy for the arts. But one longs for a true dance critic on the scene. Lack of time has prevented them from taking up invitations to observe dance classes where the real work — the laboratory work — is carried out. As a result criteria of assessing creative dance efforts fall wide of the mark. The NDTC has frequently regretted the absence of any dance critic with enough time or interest to develop the skill to criticise its work in depth. The absence of this constitutes something of a threat to sustaining high standards in the company.

There are other threats facing the company. With the dancers attaining professional standards, problems of economic security and choice between vocations can become very real. Migration to dance-centres where opportunities are likely to be greater, even if marginally so, already cuts down on the volume of work that NDTC can sustain at home. Lecture-demonstrations around the country and inter-seasonal presentations have decreased, with many of the male dancers on study-leave abroad. They return every season but there may be the chance of engagements elsewhere. The answer lies in the development of a proper National Dance Theatre School, broad-based and accessible to talents from all walks of life who can enrich the dance corps. This will provide older dancers with opportunities for lucrative teaching and for developing their choreographic and other talents. The professional dance *performer* in Jamaica seems doomed to offerings for tourist consumption of the limbo and furious fire-dances unless the government decides to make civil servants out of its dancers, or some rich private patron (an individual or a business firm) decides to indulge what will have to be for him an irresistible passion.

In the meantime, those who guide the artistic policy of the NDTC must continue in the *commitment to discovery*. Someone once said that the duty of the artist here is to 'go beneath those externals imposed by sociologist and politician, to explore the individual anguish, to plumb those unrealised wells of feeling'. Unrealised wells of feeling there certainly are: they extend, happily, beyond the acquisitive hankering after consumer goods and the myriad material fruits of technology. The sense of achievement in the expression of things of the spirit and from the inner stirrings of our own existence are in many cases considered to be just as important. Only so can we avoid the temptation of working by hearsay instead of through our own beings, and thus put the dance within the specificity of the demands that must be made upon it by time, place and exponents available. Only so can the universality which is the final test and testament be achieved. There's plenty more to be achieved and plenty more to come; the work has really just begun.

Whatever, then, may be the future of the Jamaican company in terms of survival, it cannot abandon its further commitment to excellence and its faith in the view that inherent in the collective experience of Jamaica are universal values that can be given dance-expression for the greater enrichment of the people of their country and for dance itself. Happily, chauvinism has never been allowed to assume importance over the necessity of intrinsic merit. In this there is a continuing personal responsibility for each individual artist. And here I echo the words of Edna Manley, veteran Jamaican artist and a patron of the NDTC:

> '... art for art's sake in a developing nation! What is a developing country and what makes it different? From the beginning of time the battle has raged whether the nation was young or old: art for art's sake or for the sake of the Church, or for the sake of the Royal House, or for the cause of the people, or for the aid of the politician, or for the struggle for a new idea? [Yet] deep in the heart of it all the artist *knows* that whether his art carries the burden of a philosophy ... or just sheer technique ... it is *himself* he is expressing. And the load of responsibility that he carries to society, whether a growing or a dying one, is the validity of his own being.'

This, we in the Jamaican dance-theatre — whatever our roots, whatever our rhythms — cannot afford ever to forget. For isn't the validity of one's own being the measure of one's own liberation?

**RING HUNT**

Yvonne daCosta
Audley Butler

Bert Rose
Patsy Ricketts

Barry Moncrieffe
Yvonne daCosta

Yvonne daCosta
Rex Nettleford

# THE 'KING' MUST DIE

Dorothy Sanguinetti
Yvonne daCosta
Bridget Casserly
Gertrude Sherwood
Beverly Kitson

Audley Butler
Barry Moncrieffe
Carol Miller

Yvonne daCosta
Rex Nettleford

Carol Miller
Dennis Scott
Barry Moncrieffe
Jackie Guy
Rex Nettleford

Audley Butler
Barry Moncrieffe
Rex Nettleford
Jackie Guy
Dennis Scott

# THE 'KING' MUST DIE

Patsy Ricketts
Audley Butler

Dennis Scott
Bert Rose
Barry Moncrieffe

**BACH, BRUBECK & COMPANY**

# LEGENDARY LANDSCAPE

Dennis Scott
Pansy Hassan

Carol Miller
Cheryl Ryman

# FOLK FORM

# THE REPERTOIRE

## Works Choreographed by REX NETTLEFORD

### AFRICAN SCENARIO (1962)
A young girl enters maturity and is betrothed. Her young spouse is taken off to war. She invokes the gods for his safety and he is returned to her in triumph and rejoicing. The setting is African.

*Music*  Traditional West African songs and rhythms arranged by Rex Nettleford
*Decor*  Eddy Thomas

### POCOMANIA (1963)
A highly emotional religious cult which was once outlawed in Jamaica. The dance portrays a *poco* festival with Shepherds (leaders) and their flock who travel through the spirit world in worship.

*Music*  Traditional poco tunes arranged by Nettleford
*Decor*  Rex Nettleford (1963)
Leichman (1968)

### PLANTATION REVELRY (1963)
Two young Jamaican ladies of quality (Miss Amelia and Miss Joan) return from finishing school in England and are greeted by plantation friends and workers. The songs and dances are of the nineteenth century and show off the old country jig, bucking (butting) fight, the calembe (stick fight), the set girls (rival gangs of female dandies) and John Canoe (Christmas mummers)

*Music*  Traditional Jamaican songs and rhythms collected by Nettleford
Arranged by Mapletoft Poulle
*Decor*  Eddy Thomas
(Additional dances by Eddy Thomas.
Costumes after Belisario)

### DIALOGUE FOR THREE (1963)
Three people are caught up in the eternal struggle and the Man is helpless in the face of the female force — for it is the Woman who decides.

*Music*  Joaquin Rodrigo — 'Concierto de Aranjuez'
(Guitar Concerto) 2nd movement
*Decor*  Eugene Hyde (1963)
Howard Parchment (1967)

### GALLANDAR LA PAVA (1963)
— or squiring the turkey-hen. Spanish West Indian suite.

*Music*  Traditional Colombian collected by Orford St John
Arranged by Mapletoft Poulle

### TWO DRUMS FOR BABYLON (1964)
A Young Woman on the eve of her wedding loses her loved one who is lured by phantom forces away from what he comes to regard as a Babylonian captivity. His promised land is the land of peace and love — the world of drums. She follows him in pursuit and confronts the faceless cultists, becomes possessed by the strange forces . . . . her loved one has second thoughts . . . .

*Music*  Piano variations by Aaron Copland;
Bongo Divertimento by Gutche
Drums Rhythms by Nettleford
*Decor*  Nettleford
(Suggested by the Jamaican Ras Tafari cargo cult)

### KAS KAS (1965)
In a backyard one person's business is everybody's business and the law sometimes helps to sort things out.

*Music*  Traditional Jamaican collected by Nettleford
Arranged by Adrian Clarke
*Decor*  Nettleford/Thomas

### RECOLLECTIONS (1965)
'. . . time knows/That bitter and sly sea . . . . ' (from Derek Walcott's poem *The Harbour*)

*Music*  Norman Dello Joio 'Theme and Variations'
*Decor*  Nettleford
(successor to *Diarist in Sand* — a solo)

### DANCE ANDANTE (1965)
*Music*  Schubert — 'Quintet in A Major'
*Decor*  LaYacona/Carter

### MASQUES OF GOD (1966)
The story of a Spinster and emasculated Bachelor, a Young Husband fleeing the bondage of union with a fertile Wife, two Young Lovers faced with the loss of innocence, and a Clown . . . . . . They all wear masks and search for themselves.

*Music*  Bartok/Prokofiev/Bartok
*Decor*  Howard Parchment

### MISA CRIOLLA (1967)
A theatre commemoration of the Supreme Sacrifice in moods of penitence, joy, faith, reverence and sacrifice. The episodes — Kyrie, Gloria, Credo, Sanctus, Agnus Dei.

*Music*  Creole Mass for soloists, chorus and orchestra by Ariel Ramirez
*Decor*  Howard Parchment
(Performed in Scots Kirk, Kingston at Easter 1968. Dedicated to Richmond Barthe, the sculptor)

### FOLKFORM (1968)
I. Work II. Coquette III. Courtship IV. Dance

*Music*  Traditional West Indian Arranged by Marjorie Whylie
*Decor & Costumes*  Moira Small

### THE 'KING' MUST DIE (1968)
Some will admit, at times, that men need 'kings'. If not created, then these kings are born. This makes 'queenmothers' or kingmakers out of womenfolk. We worship them — the kings that is — then help them nicely on to Calvary

*Music*  Art Blakey — 'The African Beat' (Selections)
*Decor & Costumes*  Howard Parchment

## Works Choreographed by EDDY THOMAS

### LEGEND OF LOVERS' LEAP (1962)
The story is that of Ako and Liza, two slaves who dared to fall in love against the threats of Liza's master who desired her, as he did his 'housekeepers' (the nineteenth century Jamaican euphemism for mistress).

*Music*  Oswald Russell 'Legend of Lovers' Leap' (for two pianos and later for orchestra, a commissioned work)
*Decor*  Eddy Thomas

### A TIME TO REJOICE (1962)
A time to dance is a time to rejoice

*Music*  Oswald Russell — 'A Time To Rejoice' (a commissioned work)
*Decor*  Eddy Thomas (1962)
Moira Small (1967)

### FOOTNOTES IN JAZZ (1962)
*Music*  Brubeck/Bernstein
*Decor*  Eddy Thomas

### GAMES OF ARMS (1963)
A commentary on the world situation. The venue is a schoolyard at recess time. The rival gangs are typical. Like children, like adults — the story is all the same.

*Music*  Oswald Russell 'Games of Arms' (commissioned work)
*Decor*  Milton Harley

### AND IT CAME TO PASS   (1964)
Based on the simple — and great — story of the birth of the Babe in Bethlehem. The dance chronicle runs as follows: Prologue; the Messenger and the Maiden; the Philosophers' Conference; the King at Court; No Room in the Inn; the Messenger and the Shepherds; the Birth; the King in Joy and Torment; the Adoration.
*Music*  Darius Milhaud
 'Suite Provençal'
*Decor*  Eddy Thomas

### CONCERT SUITE   (1964)
*Music*  Lennox Berkeley
 'Preludes'
*Decor*  Eddy Thomas

### COUNTRY WEDDING   (1964)
Country bride and groom — and their friends — live it up in abandoned gaiety
*Music*  Traditional
 Arranged by Mapletoft Poulle
*Decor*  Eddy Thomas
 (additional dance 'Dance Time in Cascade' created by Joyce Campbell)

### PARADE, KINGSTON 13   (1965)
A day in the life of Zone 13 in the city
*Music*  Eddy Thomas
 'Parade, Kingston 13'
 Arranged by Mapletoft Poulle
*Decor*  Lloyd van Pitterson

### JAMAICAN PROMENADE   (1966)
Suite of dances — Promenade, Boys' Dance, Plontonnade
*Music*  Traditional and original composition by Eddy Thomas. Arranged by Adrian Clarke
*Additional dance*  by Rex Nettleford (Boys' Dance)
 Eyrick Darby (Plontonnade)

### OMEGAN PROCESSION   (1966)
In the beginning, Alpha. The world turns and the Procession wends its way further and further towards Omega.
*Music*  Darius Milhaud
 'La Creation du Monde'
*Decor*  Moira Small

## Works Choreographed by
## SHEILA BARNETT

### JAZZ FANTASIA   (1963)
Based on a poem by Carl Sandburg
Poem read by Sheila Barnett

### FOILED ENCOUNTER   (1964)
*Music*  George Gershwin
 'Concerto in F'
*Decor*  John Coke

### HOMECOMING   (1966)
Sometimes a woman must wait all evening for her man to come from the fields....
*Music*  Anatol Liavov
 'Kikimora'
*Scenario*  Dennis Scott

### RING HUNT   (1968)
A dance for two. 'Tis Hobson's choice — take that or none' (Thomas Ward)
*Music*  Charlie Mingus
 'Soul Fusion' (The Black Saint and the Sinner Lady)
*Decor*  Tom Cook
*Costumes*  Sheila Barnett

## Works Choreographed by
## NEVILLE BLACK

### RITES   (1965)
I. Invocation II. Earth III. Sacrifice
*Music*  Revueltas — 'Sensemaya'
*Decor*  Neville Black, Billy duMont
*Costumes*  Neville Black (1965)
 Billy duMont (1968)

### WALTZ SUITE   (1965)
*Music*  Prokofiev
 'Midnight Waltz' from Cinderella Ballet Suite

### THE AWAKENING   (1966)
A tale of two lovers
*Music*  Stan Kenton
*Decor*  Neville Black

### NIGHT SHELTER   (1967)
The old night penny-shelters in Jamaica provided inexpensive accommodation for the countrywomen coming to town to sell their produce—but not for men who were housed elsewhere. One female breaks the 'no-males-allowed' rule with dire consequences.
*Music*  Traditional
 Arranged by Ernest Ranglin
*Decor*  Neville Black

### SONATA   (1967)
*Music*  Hindemith — 'Sonata, No.2'
*Decor & Costumes*  Neville Black

### FABLES   (1967)
After James Thurber. I. The Seal Who Became Famous II. The Little Girl and the Wolf III. The Pane of Glass in the Field IV. The Unicorn in the Garden.
*Music*  Various
*Decor & Costumes*  Susan Alexander
*Narrators*  Sheila Barnett, Neville Black

### BACH CHORALE, AVE VERUM
*Music*  Bach — 'St Matthew Passion'
 Mozart — 'Ave Verum'
 performed in Scots Kirk, Kingston
 at Easter 1968

### NEGRO SPIRITUAL   (1968)
(Work in progress)
*Music*  Negro Spiritual
 'Every Time I Feel the Spirit' performed with *Bach Chorale* on Human Rights Day 1968 — National Arena, Kingston.

### LEGENDARY LANDSCAPE   (1968)
'We have our seas full of sun, we have our trees full of leaves, morning and night we go back and forth between our seas and our trees full of nothingness.... we have our love and our death, we have our nothingness' Orhan Veli Kanik
*Music*  Electronic score compiled by Neville Black from scores by Mimaroglu, Luening, Babbit, Drukman, Berio
*Decor & Costumes*  Moira Small

### BACH, BRUBECK & COMPANY (1968)
*Music*  Bach/Brubeck
*Costumes*  Moira Small

## OTHER WORKS

### AFRO-WEST INDIAN SUITE
*Choreography*  Eryck Darby (Plontonnade)
 Rex Nettleford (Gee Bongo Lay)
 Lavinia Williams (Danse Juba)
 Eddy Thomas (Bandana Dance)
 Joyce Campbell (Dance Time in Cascade)
*Music*  Traditional
*Decor*  Moira Small

### FRENCH WEST INDIAN SUITE
*Choreography*  Eryck Darby (Santa Foulle)
 Lavinia Williams (Le Contre Danse)
*Music*  Traditional

---

*All lighting design by George Carter*
*Costume design by Eddy Thomas*
*unless otherwise stated*

## ABOUT THE AUTHORS

**REX NETTLEFORD,** who wrote the text, is one of the most remarkable young men in the West Indies. Imagine a versatility that encompasses within the skills of one man the Artistic Director, a major choreographer and a principal dancer in the Jamaica National Dance Theatre Company. Simultaneously he is the Director of the Trade Union Education Institute and of the Adult Education programme at the University of the West Indies. In the world of dance, it is not an overstatement to say that he has created a new and sophisticated dance idiom rooted in Jamaican folk culture and transformed by the disciplines of modern creative dance technique into a style and form that are an important landmark in Jamaica's discovery of herself. As a teacher of union delegates, shop stewards and organisers he is, almost miraculously, equally effective and original. And as if all these were not enough he finds time to be a member of Statutory Boards, an Industrial Relations arbitrator, a political commentator on Jamaican radio and television, a producer of plays and Jamaican musicals, an editor and an author. In the light of the totality of his contemporary achievement it seems to be an almost minor episode of his life that he should have been a Rhodes Scholar!

(MNM)

**MARIA LaYACONA,** who once worked as a free-lance photographer in New York, originally hailed from Ohio, USA. She is now a naturalised Jamaican who is well-known in her adopted country for some of the best commercial and art photography that the island has seen. This has won her several awards in the annual competitions sponsored by the Government Festival Commission. Over the past five years, largely through her association with the Jamaica National Dance Theatre Company, she has raised the level of theatre photography to unprecedented levels of excellence and is now sought after by most theatre groups. She comes from a background of sound professional experience, having worked with *Time* and *Life* and with Cinerama's production of *Seven Wonders of the World* as a still photographer. A magazine assignment to the West Indies to cover Test cricket attracted her back to Jamaica where she has been working for the past ten years. She comes from a family of photographers — her father and brother being the other two prominent members who share her profession.

(RMN)

## ACKNOWLEDGEMENTS

*Dance and Dancers*, Jan 1964 pp 30ff, Nov 1965 pp 20ff; *Dancing Times* Sept 1965 pp 617ff; *Sun Over the West Indies* — programme brochure of Jamaican Singers and Dancers 1961; *Jamaica National Dance Theatre Company*, programme brochures 1962–68; *Daily Gleaner*, Sunday Gleaner — Kingston Jamaica, editorial Oct 19, 1965; articles by Barbara Gloudon et al, crits by Norman Rae, W.E.R., Harry Milner 1962–68; *The Star*, Kingston Jamaica — editorials & articles, crits by Archie Lindo 1962 – 68; *Public Opinion*, Kingston Jamaica, crits by J. E. B. 1962 – 68; *Ballet Today* Nov 1965 pp 16–17; *Daily Express* (UK) crit by John Foster Sept 24, 1965; *Times* (London) crit Sept 25, 1965; *Daily Telegraph* (UK) crit by A.V. Coton Sept 24, 1965; *Daily Worker* (UK) crit by Jane King Sept 25, 1965; *Daily Mail* (UK) crit by Oleg Kerensky Sept 24, 1965; *The Guardian* (UK) crit by James Kennedy Sept 24, 1965; *The Recorder* crit by John Percival Oct 23, 1965; *Sunday Telegraph* (UK) crit by Nicholas Dromgoole Sept 26, 1965; Sunday Times (UK) crit by Richard Buckle Oct 3, 1965; *Liverpool Post* (UK) crit Sept 24, 1965; *Jewish Chronicle* crit Oct 1, 1965; *What's On in London* (UK) crit by Peter Noble Oct 1, 1965; *Kitchener Waterloo Record* crit by Betty Lou Lee Aug 14, 1963; *The Telegram* (Toronto) crit by George Kidd Aug 24, 1963; *Toronto Globe and Mail* crit by Herb Whittaker Aug 24, 1963; *Ontario Intelligencer* crit by Robert Tanner Aug 26, 1963; *Montreal Star* crit by Sidney Johnson Aug 27, 1963; *Reflections on the NDTC* — George Beckford, *Reply to Reflection* ........; *Jamaican Music and Jamaican Dance* by Pamela O'Gorman (NDTC Newsletter No. 4); *African Dance* — by Dermot Hussey (NDTC Newsletter No. 4); *Art for Whose and What Sake* — letter from Edna Manley to Rex Nettleford 1968; unpublished poem — 'Dialogue For Three' — by Mervyn Morris, Kingston Jamaica; *The Writer and Society* article by Winston Hackett in "Moko" No. 4,1968.

The authors wish to thank Miss Yvonne daCosta for her research work on the NDTC photographic records, Mrs Mildred Brooks, Mrs Gloria Burke and Mrs Doreen Barrow for typing the manuscript, Mr Michael Manley for his biography of one the authors and Mr Mike Henry for his general assistance and advice in the preparation of the entire book.